This book belongs to:

Alison (age 23)

Affirmations 1-5

1. I am guided by Allah’s wisdom in every step I take.

2. My Strength comes from my faith in Allah.

3. I am grateful for the countless blessings in my life.

4. Allah’s love surrounds me and protects me.

5. Every challenge I face is an opportunity to grow closer to Allah.

Affirmations 6-10

6. I am a reflection of Allah's mercy and compassion.

7. With patience and prayer, I can overcome any obstacle.

8. I trust in Allah's plan for me, knowing it is always for my best.

9. My heart finds peace in the remembrance of Allah.

10. I embrace my role as a Muslim woman with pride and dignity.

Affirmations 11-15

11. My actions today are a testimony to my faith.

12. I am committed to seeking knowledge and growing in my Deen.

13. Allah's wisdom is my guide in every decision I make.

14. My prayers are always heard by Allah, and I trust His response.

15. I am at peace, knowing that Allah is always with me.

Affirmations 16-20

16. I strive to be a source of light and kindness to those around me.

17. Allah's mercy is greater than any of my worries or fears.

18. I am grateful for the strength Allah gives me to face each day.

19. I choose faith over fear, knowing Allah is in Control.

20. My worth is defined by my faith, not by the world's standards.

Affirmations 21-25

21. I am confident in my abilities, knowing they are gifts from Allah.

22. I find joy in the simple blessings Allah has given me.

23. My heart is filled with gratitude for the love of Allah.

24. I am committed to spreading peace and kindness wherever I go.

25. I trust in Allah's timing for all things in my life.

Affirmations 26-30

26. I am empowered by the strength and guidance of Allah.

27. I seek to embody the qualities of patience, humility, and gratitude.

28. I am proud of my identity as a Muslim woman.

29. I find comfort in the Quran and Sunnah as my guides.

30. I am at peace with where I am in my journey, trusting Allah's plan.

Affirmations 31-35

31. I strive to be a better Muslim every day, with Allah as my guide.

32. My heart is a vessel for Allah's love and compassion.

33. I find strength in my faith during challenging times.

34. I am grateful for the beauty and blessings of each new day.

35. I am committed to being a positive influence in my community.

Affirmations 36-40

36. I trust that Allah's wisdom guides my decisions and actions.

37. I am confident in my faith, knowing it is my greatest strength.

38. I seek forgiveness from Allah, knowing He is the Most Merciful.

39. My prayers are a source of . peace and strength

40. I am proud of my modesty and the value it represents.

Affirmations 41-45

41. I trust in Allah's plan for my life, even when I don't understand it.

42. I strive to live each day with kindness, compassion, and gratitude.

43. I am grateful for the guidance and wisdom of the Quran.

44. My heart is at peace, knowing that Allah is always with me.

45. I choose to be patient, knowing that Allah's timing is perfect.

Affirmations 46-50

46. I am committed to learning and growing in my faith.

47. I find joy in serving others and spreading goodness.

48. I trust that Allah's plan for me is greater than I can imagine.

49. I seek to embody the qualities of the Prophet Muhammad (PBUH).

50. I am confident in my faith and proud of my Muslim identity.

Affirmations 51-55

51. I am grateful for the blessings of family, health, and faith.

52. I find strength in the support and love of my fellow Muslims.

53. I trust in Allah's wisdom to guide me through life's challenges.

54. I am committed to living a life of gratitude and humility.

55. My faith is my foundation, and I am grounded in it.

Affirmations 56-60

56. I am proud of my faith and the values it represents.

57. I seek to live each day with sincerity, kindness, and gratitude.

58. I trust in Allah's mercy and forgiveness, no matter my mistakes.

59. I am grateful for the strength and resilience that my faith gives me.

60. I strive to be a source of light and love for those around me.

Affirmations 61-65

61. I am committed to my faith and to growing closer to Allah.

62. My heart is filled with gratitude for the countless blessings Allah has given me.

63. I find peace in knowing that Allah is always with me.

64. I am proud of my identity as a Muslim woman and the values I uphold.

65. I trust in Allah's plan for me, even when the path is unclear.

Affirmations 66-70

66. I am grateful for the guidance and strength that Allah provides.

67. I seek to live a life of purpose and faithfulness to Allah.

68. I am committed to being a source of positivity and kindness.

69. I trust in Allah's wisdom and timing for all things in my life.

70. I am grateful for the support and love of my family and friends.

AFFIRMATIONS 71-75

71. I find strength in my prayers and trust in Allah's mercy.

72. I am confident in my ability to overcome challenges with faith.

73. I seek to be a reflection of Allah's love and compassion.

74. I trust that Allah's plan for me is always for my highest good.

75. I am proud of my faith and the guidance it provides me.

Affirmations 76-80

76. I am committed to living a life of kindness, humility, and guidance.

77. I find peace in the remembrance of Allah.

78. I trust in Allah's mercy and seek His forgiveness.

79. I am grateful for the strength and courage Allah gives me.

80. Through Allah all things are possible.

Printed in Great Britain
by Amazon

59295038R00020